B.R.E.A.T.H.E.

B.R.E.A.T.H.E.

Empowered To Live A Stress-Free Life

OBIOMA MARTIN

Published in the United States by OmazingYou Publishing, Pennsylvania.
Edited by Sharai Robbin & Designed by Good Ground Literary Services, LLC.

Library of Congress Cataloging -in- Publication Data Martin, Obioma
B.R.E.A.T.H.E.- Empowered to Live a Stress-Free Life/Obioma Martin
1. Spiritual Life

ISBN-13: 978-0-692-07697-2
Printed in the United States of America

10 9 8 7 6 5 4 3 2 1

FOREWORD

My introduction to Obioma was at the sounds of weeping, wailing and sobbing. It was a workshop that I attended some years ago where I heard a release from her that I will forever remember.

I do know that - in that second, at that hour - whatever was going on in her world, a personal transformation took place and the wounded Obioma was revived - emerging as a confident, bodacious, and intelligent soul.

Obioma, a pioneer and trailblazer in the field of personal empowerment and self-help, has led hundreds of women down a path of self-discovery in the midst of painful situations.

A daughter, a mother of five, and an extraordinary woman of faith and valor now takes you on a journey of her own story, sparing none of the pain but rejoicing in the resiliency. Although the key characters are not you and me, you may see reflections of your own life story in each chapter.

BREATHE is an oasis of purity, transparency, anger, peace and surrender, sharing and teaching empowering principles to use when facing your own life changing events. Each chapter provides an opportunity to do something that seems so simple, but yet difficult when life's troubles seem to be getting the best of you. BREATHE allows you to simply do just that.....take a deep breath (do it now), and BREATHE.

Obioma's work makes you want to believe in believing again.

So much labor and love has gone into this masterpiece. I pray that after each chapter, you too, will begin to learn how to simply take a deep breath and...........BREATHE.

Dr. Deshawnda Williams
On The Right Track With Dr. Dee

The world needs dreamers and the world needs doers, but most of all, the world needs dreamers that do!!!
Dr. Deshawnda Williams, MSW, M.Ed, DMin

FOREWORD

B.R.E.A.T.H.E. has been written to be a tool to break generational strongholds that hold women bound to brokenness. Each page fills Women's lungs with the breath of truth from God's Word and unapologetically gives them space to exhale their God given, identity - rewriting broken narratives and releasing a fresh truth. Obioma's story lays the backdrop for her passion and goes beyond textbook knowledge for life changing strategies. It extends approaches from real life experiences that have been tested and proven in victory over trials. She shares real- life stories that show the potential healing power of drawing closer to God and living on purpose, showcasing times where potential was both fulfilled and lost. This book challenges women to keep breathing and walking, even in the face of immense pain. As she shares in the opening pages, you will see yourself on various pages of her story and the most powerful moments are ones when you are able to use the book as a mirror not to just your past but a reflection of a no limits future. With the instructions on how to Believe, Relax, Embrace, Accept, Take Action, Heal, and Elevate, readers will learn how to build their confidence and capacity for being who they have been placed on this planet to be.

Dr. Veirdre Jackson

"B.R.E.A.T.H.E. is such an easy read that you could literally read it in a day. However, reading it a day will be a disservice as the book is written to take you on a journey of healing - healing for you as well as anyone in your circle of influence. Each chapter summarizes a B.R.E.A.T.H.E. principle brought to life by Obioma's life story and provides practical application, prayer, and scripture references for the reader.

As I read the book, I could easily recall situations in my own life that have left me unable to breathe, literally. Through reading this book, Go d has confirmed for me that in order to experience true healing, I am going to have dig deep. I am going to have to go there and unearth the experiences of my 7-year-old, my 11-year-old, and my 17-year-old selves. I have always been reluctant to revisit the roots of those experiences; afraid of what I would feel. I am not afraid anymore. I have a blue print.

Obioma's transparency is refreshing and will undoubtedly be the catalyst for change for those who not only read it, but do the work required. I for one will, as Obioma says, "make the conscious decision to B.R.E.A.T.H.E."

-Gail Kennedy

"I must say that this book has kept my eyes glued to the pages. Mrs. Martin poured out her soul in this book and as a woman who's been through similar issues, it was refreshing to experience her vulnerability and transparency. This book is a tool for transformation and is much need for all women. I only have five words after reading this book, "Honey, I'm ready to BREATHE!"

– Shanital Vital Davis

"Raw vulnerability, exposing her hidden and once felt shame with a gentle honesty that is breathtaking. Obioma's B.R.E.A.T.H.E is a succinct and poignant transformation filled experience that every woman should digest and apply where the application is needed.

An intersection of personal transformation and a Christian woman's guide to loving yourself through and beyond divorce, this book should go on more than your "good reads list," you need it in your war room!"

- Naketa R. Thigpen

Life happens. Life happens to everyone in various ways and times and although each individual experiences the uniqueness of life differently, through Obioma's B.R.E.A.T.H.E. journey we no longer have to experience it alone nor without a guide. Obioma Martins' B.R.E.A.T.H.E. journey is an eye opening, thought provoking, first-hand account that guides the hand of the reader as he/she applies the steps that will bring them through a period of trial to a place of healing. It's not easy and she digs deep, revealing all the "stuff" we often leave buried, but I promise you Obioma's story will make you cry, become angry and rejoice in triumph as you recognize and relate to a story that could be your own. Who is this book for? Who is the intended audience? To put it bluntly if you have lived through, going through or will go through some things then this book is for you. That should encompass everyone. So I implore you to take this journey as you reflect, do the work and come to same conclusion I did and that is it time for me to B.R.E.A.T.H.E.

-Stephanie West

Acknowledgements

Thank you to my phenomenal editor, literary coach and overall amazing super friend and sister in Christ, Sharai Robbin. Thank you, Gail Kennedy and Stephanie West, for supporting me and being a part of my team. Thank you to every women who was a part the first two B.R.E.A.T.H.E. challenges. Thank you to Victoria Marie, Diana Hill and Laverne Cheeseboro for encouraging me along the way and sharing your stories. Thank you to Ulicia Lawrence for hosting the monthly B.R.E.A.T.H.E. empowerment circles. Thank you to the Juvenile Justice Center for allowing me to host and facilitate B.R.E.A.T.H.E. mentoring circles for the youth. Thank you everyone who supported me, showed up on my FB lives, showed me love, and shared my stories. Thank you to Teanna Lanise, my graphic designer, for being amazing. Thank you to my B.R.E.A.T.H.E. ambassadors: Shanita Vital Davis, Dr. Kreslyn Kelley-Ellis, Tihanna McCleese, Jacquie Carter, Diamond Williams. My B.R.E.A.T.H.E. prayer group: Sonya Delotch, Dr. Veirde Jackson, Peggy McManus, Cheryl Hurley, Dr. Deshawnda Williams, Nephetina Serrano, Twanda Sanders-Williams, Bridget Cunnigham, and Michelle Govan. Thank you Sereda Thompson for sharing your story. Thank you, Zenita Slaughter, for loving on me through FB consistently every day throughout this journey. Thank you, Michelle Snow, Cynthia Allen, Quisha Thompson, Johnna Ithier, Erica Polk, Almitra Tankersly, Aliya Johnson, Bertina Pelzer, Lougenia Rucker, Tonie McDougal, and Naketa Thigpen for always giving me wise counsel, and being a listening ear. Thank you, Tara Coney, for being my ride or die. Thank you, Danielle Paige Jeter, for being my tour manager and PR person.

DEDICATION

This book is dedicated to women everywhere, young and mature. It is my desire to help women get unstuck in every area of their lives and remove the barriers that prevent them from breathing and enjoying life.

To my one and only daughter Jael Maxwell, my mother, Gloria A. Brown, my sisters, every student, mentee, and client, this book is for you. I listened to your stories, to your struggles, and your journey. This book is for you.

CONTENTS

Introduction xiii

Chapter 1   B – Believe 1
Chapter 2   R – Release...9
Chapter 3   E – Embrace... 19
Chapter 4   A – Accept..27
Chapter 5   T – Take Action 35
Chapter 6   H – Heal...51
Chapter 7   E – Elevate 61

Final Words For The Journey...71
About the Author 75

INTRODUCTION

B.R.E.A.T.H.E is a journey about continuous self-development. I'm writing this book to share my journey with you: my journey of doubt, self-esteem, suicide, faith, hope, love, and elevation. Learning how to B.R.E.A.T.H.E. allowed me to see the innermost parts of myself and understand my battles with depression and trying to be a superwoman for everyone, but myself. My journey is not unique. I am confident that you will see yourself as I share my experiences and you will be able to identify those places in you that can use some developing. So, take this journey with me and in the end you will be empowered to stand up, stand out, advocate for yourself, walk in your purpose, walk in your calling, and most importantly live a stress free life!

I will walk you through seven principles I applied to my life in hopes that you'll be able to apply these same principles to your own circumstances. The first principle is Believe. You must believe in yourself. As women of all colors, sizes, and shapes we can't hide from the pressure of trying to be beautiful according to the status quo, social media, and society. In this first chapter, you'll understand and begin to identify your own struggle, lies you have believed about yourself, and learn strategies to overcome the pressure of the world through the Word of God. You will also find scriptures along the way to use as a foundation and anchor in understanding who you are according to God's Word and as reminders of how God has a master plan for your life. I encourage you to use these scriptures daily as you take this journey.

The second principle we will explore is Release and Relax. I'll share with you how I had to release people, places, and things that were toxic in my life so that I could relax and enjoy the fruits of my labor.

This step sounds a bit difficult, but trust me it can be done. I'll walk you through every step. The third principle is Embrace and here we'll focus on embracing the new you. I want you to get excited about this new season you're walking into. Your life is getting ready to change for the better as you move through this journey.

The fourth principle is Accepting. We have to accept who we are first, and then work to accept situations we cannot change. This chapter will help you accept your past and move forward with what you can change and work to be at peace with the things you can't. The fifth principle is Take Action. We must get control over our own lives by taking action and stop trying to change and control the lives of others. We'll cover eight areas of your life that you can take control of today and start to see major changes.

The sixth principle is Healing. You cannot move forward in life broken, still dealing with the emotional pain of the past. You'll learn practical, easy to apply tactics in order to really heal and move into a new place of peace in your life. The seventh principle is Elevation. After you have applied the other six principles, it is time for you to elevate your life, your business, your finances, and your relationships. Use this chapter to gear up and push through to a new way of abundant living.

I am confident, that upon the completion of reading this book, you will be empowered to look in the mirror and face your fears. This journey is about taking back your life and owning what God has for you and the blessings He has placed over your life. Be empowered to believe in yourself. Be empowered to release, embrace, accept, take action, heal, and ultimately elevate.

Chapter

1

B *– Believe*

Why are names so important? Have you ever pondered on how your name is connected to how you see yourself and what you believe about yourself? Back in Bible days, the name a child was given was connected to their destiny, their purpose, and their lineage. I was my mother's miracle baby girl; my mom was told she would never have children due to physical abuse she received at the hand of her mother. Unmarried and alone, my mother had me by way of C-section since she could not push and I went without a name for three days.

After being in the hospital nameless for some time my mother decided to name me Obioma, one of three names that had been suggested to her by a Nigerian friend of her brother's. It was the only one she could spell and pronounce. Unfortunately for me, she was the only one who could. Names carry a lot of weight and it was rough growing up when no one could say my name right. I was teased, talked about, and bullied. My peers, teachers, family members, and friends stumbled over my name and I became the butt of everyone's jokes. I was mistreated and abused all because of my name. Kids were brutal, always teasing and mocking me, but the adults were worse. They flat-out called me Oats, Oatmeal, Obi-Wan Kenobi, Olive Oil, and the list goes on. I was always made fun of. No one ever spoke to me kindly or told me that I was beautiful or valuable. I didn't feel good about myself and I didn't feel accepted. Consequently, when it came to what I thought about me, the word "beautiful" was never a part of the conversation.

I didn't grow up believing I was beautiful, or even valuable. Truth is, I had no clear perception of myself. My own name caused confusion and as a result, I allowed the thoughts and opinions of others to validate what I thought about myself. Now, looking back on my childhood, I realize the village I grew up in shaped my self-perception to a considerable extent.

When a girl grows up in an environment where everyone celebrates you by telling you how beautiful you are, or how pretty you look, it boosts your self-esteem and confidence. Growing up in the opposite manner, I had constant feelings of inadequacy that caused me to lower my standards and attempt to blend in just so that I could fit in. Inadequacy caused me to accept whatever others offered me, be it male or female. I did not believe in myself because I did not see myself as being beautiful and it all started with my name.

I was ashamed of, not only my name, but also how I looked. I didn't have any curves, or a "nice frame" like the other girls my age that the boys were always drawn to. You know the girls with big butts, big breasts, long hair and nice smooth skin? Yeah, and all those pretty girls had pretty names like Sherry, Lisa, and Nicole. No one had ever heard of a tall, skinny, and frail Obioma.

As I was entering into my teenage years, I was determined to escape my name. We moved from South Philadelphia to Germantown when I was around twelve or thirteen years old, going into the seventh grade, and I told everyone I met from that point on, that my name was Shadia Luv. Shadia was the alias name that I borrowed from my favorite cousin, Angie, at the time. Shadia Luv made me believe in myself. It was almost as if the past was behind me and I had a brand new start in life. I felt confident about who I was and how I looked. Shadia Luv was sexy, appealing, and a lot easier to pronounce. I liked being called Shadia way more than I liked people stumbling and stuttering over Obioma. I carried the name Shadia Luv until I graduated high school. After graduation, I landed my first job at John Wanamakers retail clothing store as summer help in the stockroom. Wanamakers was my first government job and I could no longer use my alias. I had to start using the name that was on my birth certificate. I remember receiving my first paycheck and I thought, *This is it. It's time for people to start putting some respect on my name.*

As I entered adulthood and began to network and meet other professionals at various events, people started asking me if my name had a meaning or if I was from Africa. I became intrigued by the interest people took over the uniqueness of my name.

I ended up working with someone who was from Nigeria and she would tell me stories pertaining to the meaning of my name. In Nigeria, Igbo tribe, Obioma means grace, goodness and favor. The literal meaning being, "good heart." I also found that Obioma is identified as a noble street tailor in Africa. Many Queens and Kings of Africa carried the name Obioma. I learned that my name is not only beautiful, but it's also powerful. I came to understand the value in who I was and I was able to begin to believe in myself by just discovering the meaning of my name. I am very proud of my name now and I exude confidence when I introduce myself as Obioma Martin.

Believing in yourself is also knowing that you are beautiful, even when no one tells you. Unfortunately, the startling fact is that only a small percentage of women describe themselves as beautiful. After reflecting on the lies women have been told regarding society's narrow definition of beauty, we are left with the task of defining beauty for ourselves. But, it's important to remember that beauty is only skin deep and my definition of beauty speaks to who I am and the values I maintain as an individual. Beauty is not about your name, weight, height, or facial features. It starts on the inside and what is displayed on the outside. I am patient, strong, determined, brilliant, funny, sweet, loving, kind, and passionate. These are the characteristics that make me beautiful. Not to disregard the physical because you have to love your physical beauty also and I love my eyes, my smile, my curves, and my confidence. These are the things that make me love my body and my brown skin. Every scar, crack, dimple, and blemish is beauty and they all come together to make me beautiful.

My mother often tells me how, as a teenager, she had to look herself in the mirror every day and say positive affirmations because she did not get it from her mother or her village. Her mother, my grandmother, was verbally and physically abusive. Today, my heart hurts when I hear adults talk negatively about children's appearances as if they can change the way they look. The truth is that beauty is in the eye of the beholder. My beautiful may not be yours and that is okay, because I love me. To be in a place and space to appreciate the diversity of the beauty of others, we must start to embrace who we really are. Today, I am in a place in my life where I love all of me. I am no longer trying to blend in, fit in, or be like anyone else.

The truth is, people are always going to have something to say and there isn't much you can do about that, but when you believe in yourself, you're not worried about the opinions of others or things you can't control. Believe that you are the definition of beauty, imperfections, flaws, and all.

Proverbs 31:30 says, "Charm is deceptive, and beauty is fleeting; but a woman who fears the Lord is to be praised." This verse explains that physical beauty will fade over time, our skin and shape changes overtime, but true beauty (virtue) is timeless. This means that we can invest in our outward appearance all day long, but at the end of the day, if you have no values or virtue, such as love, joy, kindness, humility and self-control you have no beauty. Without a relationship with Christ you are unattractive.

That's because beauty isn't just one thing. Beauty is a multitude of things that go into shaping an individual like; personality, cheerfulness, compassion, leadership, service, and maintaining a positive attitude. These attributes will make a less attractive person shine and become beautiful instantly. It's like when you see someone who, for whatever reason, society wouldn't deem as attractive, but they are caring, compassionate, and genuine, and you say to yourself, "Wow, that sister is beautiful." The person who goes the extra mile for someone else even when they are struggling themselves is beautiful. Beauty is not a simple thing. It is a culmination of how we feel about ourselves and others, how we carry ourselves, how we treat ourselves, how we treat one another and, more importantly, how we serve God.

We are all beautiful. We just need to take the time to believe that we are enough, nothing broken, lacking or missing. We have to believe that God made us beautiful from the inside out and that means shutting out the influences of the world around us, and finding our inner beauty so we can breathe.

PRAYER OF BELIEF

In the name of Jesus, I walk out of the realm of failure, low self esteem, and doubt and into the arena of success, giving thanks to You. Father, You have qualified me and me, whole. Father, You have delivered and drawn me to Yourself out of the control and the dominion of darkness, failure, doubt, and fear, and have transferred me into the Kingdom of the Son of Your Love, in whom there is good success and freedom from fears, and moral conflicts. I rejoice in Jesus who has come that I might have life and have it more abundantly.

Today I submit to the Word of God. I consent and attend to Your sayings, Father. Your words shall not depart from my sight. I will keep them in the midst of my heart. For they are life and success to me, and healing and health to all my flesh. I keep my heart with all vigilance, and above all, I guard it, for out of it flows the springs of life.

Your Word exposes, sifts, analyzes and judges the very thoughts and purposes of my heart. Today I shall be transformed by the renewing of my mind, that I may prove what is the good and acceptable perfect will of God.

Today I fix my mind on whatever is true, whatever is worthy of reverence and is honorable and seemly, whatever is just, whatever is pure, whatever is lovely and loveable, whatever is kind and gracious. I ask for all of these things or better in Jesus name. Amen.

SCRIPTURE REFERENCES

3 John 2	Romans 12:2	1 Corinthians 2:16 AMP
Joshua 1:8	Proverbs 3:5,6	Proverbs 21:5
Hebrews 4:12 AMP	Philippians 4:6-8 NIV	2 Corinthians 10:4

REFLECTIONS

2

R – *Release*

Have you ever felt suffocated by a relationship? Do you often feel stifled by feelings of frustration, anger, or depression? Taking the next step in living your abundant life is letting go of everything that has held you back. It's important to no longer carry the load of unnecessary negative emotions, but release them so that you can finally B.R.E.A.T.H.E. freely and easily. Release means to allow or enable escape from confinement; to set free, permitting something or someone to move, act or flow freely.

Releasing toxic people is no easy task and can only be done through prayer and fasting. When we are not obedient to the Word of God we sacrifice ourselves physically and emotionally to unnecessary pain and heartache as a result of us holding onto people, places, and things when God has already told us to release them because they are not good for us. To B.R.E.A.T.H.E. we must first learn how to release whatever is stopping us from being free, that includes; old wounds, painful memories and toxic people.

Everything we do begins with a decision. We can decide to release things or hold on to them and allow them to fester and grow on the inside of us like a fungus causing us to be sick. We have to let it all go for our own health and well-being. I, unfortunately, learned the lesson of release the hard way.

As I mentioned before, my childhood wasn't really a warm and tender experience, but I struggled even into adulthood with negative family influences. January 1999 on an ice cold day, I had a enough of my stepfather and mother. I called my uncle James and begged him to allow me to live with him until I could get myself together. My uncle allowed me to rent a room from him that my daughter and I shared for one year. He said he was going to prepare me for marriage so that by December of 1999 I would be ready to marry. Toward the end of the year, a woman from my church prophesied over me and said that I was going to get married. I thought this was confirmation and was looking forward to who this man could possibly be with great expectation. I met the man who would soon be my husband a few weeks later at work. He was the only black manager in the IT department and he was smart as a whip. I was immediately intrigued.

I worked in Human Resources and our job had free tickets for a black tie gala. This man had been asking me out for the last three months and my answer was always I don't have time. When the opportunity to attend the gala presented itself I immediately thought of him. I had to wear a gown and he had to wear a Tuxedo. I asked him if wanted to be my date for the event. He said yes, and we had an incredible night. It was beautiful, everyone was in elegant attire. He asked me to marry him that night. Yes, on our first date! And, I said yes. That was in October. We got married on New Year's Eve and the week before we got married I found out he had a drug addiction.

I hadn't seen him in two or three days and it was revealed to me that he was homeless and living in a shelter. In addition to the suffering by way of my mother's husband, I was also helping take care of my great grandmother who was very sick and needed around the clock care. My life was in shambles. I didn't know where to go or what to do. All I knew was that my fiancé was smart. I didn't care what he had going on. He was smart, and I was going to make it work. So, I still went ahead and married him because I felt like, if nothing else, he could protect me from my stepfather and I was willing to endure whatever came with that. At twenty-one, it was better than what I was dealing with and I figured, we were going to figure it out together and we did. We did, but I endured a whole lot more than I ever truly had to because of my impatience. I'd made a list of ten qualities I wanted in a husband and my fiancé had nine out of ten. I didn't factor in the addiction and I settled for less than I deserved.

We were married for eighteen years. He consistently struggled with his addiction and would disappear in the middle of the night and sometimes for days at a time. He would spend every dollar we had, regardless if the money was for our mortgage, food, clothing, or utilities. He would miss appointments, holidays, and even special occasions with our children. I would get upset and sometimes not eat or sleep, and I suffered from daily headaches and depression. I felt heartbroken and lost.

I often thought, is this my life? My thoughts even turned to ones of suicide. I would stay up all night crying and praying consumed with thoughts of where he might be. I realized that I was unstable and insecure. Over time, I became even more of a wreck. I had to sleep with my car keys and wallet under my pillow. There was nothing in our house of any value because he sold everything that was worth anything to feed his habit. Sometimes, I would be so filled up with rage, I wanted to fight and inflict on him the pain he made me feel. I became very short and snappy with my children because I felt alone, scared and trapped, having no way of expressing what I was going through. I was so irritable, anything would trigger my fury and pain.

From the outside looking in, I looked like a superwoman, caring for my family, working for my clients, and teaching my students, but I was really hiding everything I was going through. I was on the brink of suicide every day. I was doubting myself, suffering from low self-esteem and I had no confidence in myself or my abilities. My life was falling apart. I was a battered woman and psychologically abused by my husband. His jealousy, selfishness, controlling and manipulative ways became destructive and started to deplete my self-worth. I knew, none of this was normal but I believed it was what God had planned for me.

My husband and I were not in agreement and had not been in agreement for years. We started our marriage rooted in lies and deceit. I hid the truth about his addiction from my parents and all those who cared about me. I was ashamed and embarrassed by the lies I had to tell just to save face. I'd settled but I felt it was my cross to bear so I hid my pain and refused to ask for help.

Over the course of the last five years of my marriage, I began to earnestly seek the Lord.

It was through my suffering that I began to really study the Word of God. One scripture that stood out to me was 1 Corinthians 7:15, "But if the unbelieving partner leaves, let him leave. In such cases the [remaining] brother or sister is not [spiritually or morally] bound. But God has called us to peace." (AMP). I realized then that it is not a part of the will of God for us to be in an abusive marriage or relationship with anyone.

This study of God's Word brought me closer to Him and I was better able to recognize His voice. It's here that I learned I didn't have to suffer and everything I was going through was a direct result of wanting something that God had never promised me. I wanted my marriage to work. I wanted to believe the lies. I wanted my children to grow up in a two-parent household, but not at the cost of my sanity and my well-being.

The more I sought after God, it became clearer that we were unevenly yoked according to 2 Corinthians 6:14, "Don't become partners with those who reject God. How can you make a partnership out of right and wrong? That's not partnership; that's war. Is light best friends with dark? Does Christ go strolling with the Devil? Do trust and mistrust hold hands? Who would think of setting up pagan idols in God's holy Temple?" (MSG).

The whole time it was me punishing myself when God had never joined me to this man in the first place. I was already released. I thought that God had turned his back on me because of my decision but when I spent more time with Him, I learned in his Word that He still loved me. Romans 8:38-39, says, "For I am convinced that neither death nor life, neither angels nor demons, neither the present nor the future, nor any powers, neither height nor depth, nor anything else in all creation, will be able to separate us from the love of God that is in Christ Jesus our Lord." (NIV).

I knew that I needed to release this relationship that was toxic to my physical and mental health. I began to make every move possible to set myself up to get out. I started working on my credit, investing, and attending conferences to help me expand my business. I began researching neighborhoods, schools, and looking for a new apartment for me and my children. I was scared, but things had to change. After a few months of searching, I found a place. I packed up all my clothes and the kid's clothes. We got an air mattress and moved out. The peace I felt in that empty apartment was more than words can describe. It was my release. My atmosphere had changed from toxic and negative to peaceful and serene, total quietness. I woke up to birds chirping instead of arguments and the stress of wondering what the day would bring. For the first time in over sixteen years, I could breathe.

I'd felt so weak and depleted for so long. Toxic relationships can do that to you. They can strip you of your strength and drag you and keep you down. It's like having a weight on you and every time you try to get up it feels like somebody has their feet on your back and until you really know God and allow Him to release you from those relationships you won't be able to stand. It's almost like doing a push-up and your body isn't strong enough. The muscles in your arms can't hold up the weight of your body and so even though you're trembling and you're trying to have the correct posture and your toes are aligned and your feet and your elbows are positioned the right way, because your muscles aren't strong enough to support the weight of your body, you keep falling back to the ground. That's what it feels like without God. But, God was with me when my children and I moved and I felt like I could do a push-up in my apartment.

Divorce is not easy and I'm not advocating for it, but this was what I needed in order to move forward in my life. Often, whether we like it or not, we have to release people from our lives. We need to free ourselves from damaging and unbalanced relationships. All different types of relationships we're in can be toxic and unhealthy. This can include, familial, platonic, and sexual. We tend to hold onto people because of our own insecurities and because we don't really know God. We use people to fill voids within us instead of spending time with Him. We may think we won't find anyone else to love us or that we're obligated to do things for people because they're related to us. We may even have the desire to be needed or wanted or even to be accepted, but all of this is toxic to our well-being and none of it is God.

When we hold on to people and things that we shouldn't, it affects our ability to B.R.E.A.T.H.E and be our genuine selves. We have to release people so that they can no longer hold us hostage to their toxic words or actions. As women, we are natural nurturers and caregivers because this is who God created us to be, but He never intended for us to be someone else's savior or stepping stone. In order for us to be good to anyone, we first have to learn how to be good to ourselves and that means releasing the negative people in our lives.

It was a long journey for me to get to the place of recognizing God's voice and releasing, but you don't have to endure the same pains. If you're in a situation or relationship that makes you feel trapped, isolated, and abused, seek God and let that thing go. Release everything and everyone that doesn't help propel you into the women God has called you to be. There's no need to hold onto people or things that hold you back. Release them and allow God to do a mighty work in you.

PRAYER OF RELEASE

Father, help me to meet new friends - friends who will encourage me. May I find in these friendships the companionship and fellowship You have ordained for me. I know that You are my source of love, companionship, and friendship. Your love and friendship are expressed through my relationship with You and members of the Body of Christ.

According to Proverbs 27:17, as iron sharpens iron, so friends sharpen the minds of each other. As we learn from each other, may we find a worthy purpose in our relationship. Keep me well balanced in my friendships, so that I will always please You rather than pleasing other people.

I ask for divine connections - good friendships ordained by You. Thank You for the courage and grace to release detrimental relationships. I ask and receive, by faith, discernment for developing healthy relationships. Your Word says that two are better than one, because if one falls, there will be someone to lift that person up.

Father, You know the hearts of people, so I won't be deceived by outward appearances. Bad friendships corrupt good morals. Thank You for quality relationships and surrounding me with people who help me build a stronger character and draw me closer to You.

Thank You, Lord that I can entrust myself and my need for reciprocal relationships, healthy friendships, and partnerships into Your keeping. I submit to the leadership of the Holy Spirit, and I ask for all of these things or better in Jesus name. Amen.

SCRIPTURE REFERENCES

Proverbs 13:20 NIV	1 Corinthians 15:33 AMP	Ephesians 5:30 NIV
James 1:17 NIV	Philippians 2:2,3 NIV	Proverbs 17:17
Romans 12:15	Psalm 84:11 NIV	Proverbs 18:24

REFLECTIONS

REFLECTIONS

_____

_____

_____

_____

_____

_____

_____

_____

_____

_____

_____

_____

_____

_____

_____

_____

_____

_____

_____

3

E – *Embrace*

I'm so excited about this new season in my life. There was a time that I thought I would never be anything without my husband. My total existence was in him. Once I stepped outside of him, I was able to embrace this season of newness, freedom, and liberation. The devil no longer has a hold on me because my heavenly father has set me free. All that God has promised me, it's all available to me right now. In this new season I am tasting and seeing the fruit of my labor. In the song *New Season*, Israel Houghton and Martha Munizzi sing, "The new millennium presents a new horizon and no greater time for us to make a choice and take a stand all that we need is resting safely in the Master's hand."

It's a new season. Old things have passed away. The things that used to upset you and stress you are no longer an issue. It's a new day! Decree and declare your freedom! By releasing all that old baggage, there is a fresh anointing upon you. Now, you can walk in power and prosperity because you have released all that was keeping you bound.

Romans 12:2 tells us to, "Take our everyday, ordinary lives, our sleeping, eating, going-to-work, and walking-around life—and place it before God as an offering" (MSG). Embracing what God does for you is waking up every morning and being born anew and afresh. Every day there are new things on your mind, new people to meet, and new things to do. As you wake up and start your day, there's no need to think of the past and dwell on the mistakes you made. Instead, focus on the future and what you can create.

Fix your attention on God and you'll be changed from the inside out everyday. In this new season of embracing, it's your charge to readily recognize what He wants from you, and quickly respond to it. Unlike the negative influences in the world around you, always dragging you down, God brings the best out of you. The Word of God is our GPS that guides and develops us into spiritual maturity, so we become unbothered by the distractions and detours of this world.

I don't know about you, but the old me was easily distracted and easily influenced by everything around me. I was always angry, hostile, frustrated, stressed, and anxious. I used to be a doubter, a complainer and I was extremely judgmental. I had a sharp tongue and a quick temper. My heart was hard, I was stubborn and hard-headed. The old me operated from a place of low self-esteem because I was dealing with bitterness, hurt, resentfulness and hatred. But Praise be to God, he released me from those old things, protected me from myself, and nurtured me into a new season of my life that I am fully embracing.

I stopped taking things personal and no longer looked at things or circumstances as rejection, but through God, I was able to see that hurt people hurt people, and that freed me from so much pain. God shifted my mindset and I began to think differently, focusing only on the goodness and fullness of God and his promises. This mindset shift is like children and selective awareness. Have you ever noticed how children will tune out everything around them when they're intently focused on one thing, like their cellphones, the television or their tablets? Nothing can distract them from what they've set their eyes on. This is a practice you'll have to return to in this new season of embracing. God wants you to focus on him, so he can set you free and give you the abundant life he's promised.

Matthew 11:28 -30 MSG asks, "Are you tired? Worn out? Come to me. Get away with me and you'll recover your life. I'll show you how to take a real rest. Walk with me and work with me—watch how I do it. Learn the unforced rhythms of grace. I won't lay anything heavy or ill-fitting on you. Keep company with me and you'll learn to live freely and lightly."

Also, notice how children embrace everything as a new experience? Children have a freshness and newness because they do not have the weight of the world on their shoulders. God reminds us that you don't have to carry this weight either. It can be easy to open up and embrace the new if you picture it the way God does. Remember that God wants nothing but the best for you, trust Him. Keep this picture in your mind, that the future is positive for you and it will be better than anything you have ever known.

Allowing God to handle everything allows us to focus on truly experiencing life as He has called us to. A new mindset leads to feeling alive and being fully conscious and aware of everything around you. You have to be able to step out of your comfort zone, live a little, and experience new things. Don't stay stuck in old routines because they are so familiar that you do them without even thinking. Try out new routines each day. Doing new things is invigorating to the physical body. When you're physically moving, you're more cognitively alert and aware of the world. Try bringing this same alertness to whatever you do normally to experience familiar activities in new ways. As you embrace the new, remember things are always going to get better. God does not take anything away unless something better is coming. Every down cycle is followed by a great leap forward.

In developing into the new you, you'll have to learn to balance your focus between things that require your attention while not being sidetracked by meaningless, trivial, and irrelevant distractions. As you grow and evolve, what you create will be even more joyous than what you have ever known or could even imagine.

HOW TO EMBRACE THE NEW:

- **Be joyful.** Be open to the joy of the Lord and what lies ahead today, tomorrow, or even during the next hour. The joy of the Lord is your strength.

- **Release.** Let go of any predetermined pictures of what your day might be like and experience the day fresh, allowing things to be different from what you might have expected or planned.

- **Be spontaneous.** Decide to be open to all possibilities as they unfold. Allow new, creative thoughts, activities, and experiences to come and act without hesitation.

- **Connect.** Connect with the Holy Spirit that lives on the inside of you and ask for assistance in embracing new ways of feeling, being, speaking, and acting today.

- **Explore.** Think about how you can do something you normally do in a fresh and innovative way. If you realize you are doing something out of habit, stop, connect with your innermost self, and ask to be shown a new way to act.

- **Take a break.** Pause at regular intervals throughout the day and find something you are truly grateful for. In every stressful situation, search for one thing that you can give honest thanks for. Think about the goodness of Jesus and how he died and suffered for you. He became poor, so you could be rich. He became sick so you could be healed. Think about how you awoke in your right mind. Think about your eyesight, your ability to hear, smell and taste, the mobility of your muscles, and limbs. Take a break and practice conscious positive thinking.

- **Use your senses.** Utilizing your senses helps bring awareness and clarity during a stressful or trying situation. Through what you see, what you touch, what you smell, and taste, you can embrace your current experience.

- **The start and the finish.** Use the first and last moments of your day to take stock of the positive and negative experiences. Reflect on the good things and see the negative experiences as learning and growing opportunities.

- **Daydream.** Don't fill every moment of your day with Twitter, Facebook, and YouTube. Just let yourself relax and allow your mind to wander. Be careful not to let your mind harp on the negative in these little reveries. Close your eyes and let your mind free associate, even if there are no words that accompany this state. This is like a mini holiday in the middle of the day. Small refreshing daydreaming breaks help your mind integrate lessons and recuperate.

- **Surrender.** While it can be great to set goals and visualize the future, don't let yourself get too caught up in the vision of how things "should" be. Be prepared to let go of your attachments to any particular outcome so that you can embrace something bigger than you have ever imagined. Learn that to yield does not mean that you lose. Let God lead you down unexpected turns and you will discover joy, peace, favor, and reciprocal relationships in the most unexpected places.

Embracing this new season means stepping away from the old you and tapping into the spirit of God inside of you. First Corinthians 2:14-16 says, "The unspiritual self, just as it is by nature, can't receive the gifts of God's Spirit. There's no capacity for them. They seem like so much silliness. Spirit can be known only by spirit—God's Spirit and our spirits in open communion. Spiritually alive, we have access to everything God's Spirit is doing, and can't be judged by unspiritual critics." (MSG)

Everyday I work on embracing my spirituality and my hope is that you figure out what you need to do in order to get started embracing your new season and breathing with intention.

PRAYER OF EMBRACING

Father, I thank You for clarity of mind. I thank You for clean air and healthy lungs. I thank You that I can now breath with intention because of Your Word. Your Word healed me. Your Word gave me strength to live and to fight for my life. Your Word encouraged me and empowered me to embrace my emotions so that they could be a gauge and not my guide. Father, I anticipate the good things You have prepared for me today. Bring complete order to my day and my life as I seek You first and make Your will my priority. I rejoice in the new day You have given me and I praise You for making it a healthy, peaceful, fruitful, and productive day. Thank You for teaching me ways to increase my effectiveness, take care of my physical body, decrease stress, and work smarter.

Lord, Thank You for declaring Your plans for me - plans to prosper me and not to harm me, plans to give me hope and a future. I choose to renew my mind and to embrace Your plans for my life. Teach me knowledge and good judgement. I choose to take my life - my sleeping, eating, going to work, and walking around life - and place it before You as an offering. Embracing what You do for me is the best thing I can do for You. I work according to your agenda and perform for an audience of one—the Lord Jesus Christ. In Jesus's name, Amen.

SCRIPTURE REFERENCES

Psalm 139:14	Psalm 119:66	Jeremiah 29:11
Romans 12:1 MSG	Proverbs 14:15	Philippians 1:20 AMP

REFLECTIONS

4

A – *Accept*

Have you ever been criticized, persecuted or talked about? Have you ever made a bad decision and had to accept the consequences? Have you ever been discriminated against or wrongly accused? We all go through life having to accept difficult things. We can either struggle with those difficulties or come to terms with what has happened and what will be. Most people struggle in life because they are afraid of the unknown, afraid of change, or because they are trying to change something beyond their control. When we come to terms with the fact that life is eighty percent out of our control and twenty percent in our control it's easier to accept the things you cannot control and focus on the things you can.

Our struggle with change leads us blindly by our emotions because we cannot have our way, but when we learn acceptance it allows us to see things from a different perspective. We learn that we cannot change people but we can change ourselves. We can't change what people say or what they do, but we can accept people for who they are and change how we allow their actions or decisions to affect us. How we process information and interactions with others determines how we enjoy life. The word of God teaches us how to act not react.

Romans 12:9-21 reminds us that, *"Love is to be sincere and active [the real thing—without guile and hypocrisy]. Hate what is evil [detest all ungodliness, do not tolerate wickedness]; hold on tightly to what is good. Be devoted to one another with [authentic] brotherly affection [as members of one family], give preference to one another in honor; never lagging behind in diligence; aglow in the Spirit, enthusiastically serving the Lord; constantly rejoicing in hope [because of our confidence in Christ], steadfast and patient in distress, devoted to prayer [continually seeking wisdom, guidance, and strength], contributing to the needs of God's people, pursuing [the practice of] hospitality. Bless those who persecute you [who cause you harm or hardship]; bless and do not curse [them]. Rejoice with those who rejoice [sharing others' joy], and weep with those who weep [sharing others' grief]. Live in harmony with one another; do not be haughty [conceited, self-important, exclusive], but associate with humble people [those with a realistic self-view]. Do not overestimate yourself. Never repay anyone evil for evil. Take thought for what is right and gracious and proper in the sight of everyone. If possible, as far as it depends on you, live at peace with everyone. Beloved, never avenge yourselves, but leave the way open for God's wrath [and His judicial righteousness]; for it is written [in Scripture], "Vengeance is Mine, I will repay," says the Lord. But if your enemy is hungry, feed him; if he is thirsty, give him a drink; for by doing this you will heap [a]burning coals on his head." Do not be overcome and conquered by evil, but overcome evil with good."*

As a teenager, I remember feeling alone, isolated, rejected, and unloved. I remember being at the wrong place at the wrong time, with a man who could have gone to jail for statutory rape because of our relationship. At the time, I was only fifteen and he was twenty-four. I had always been attracted to older men and I lied about my age to make myself more appealing. I remember going to see him on my sixteenth birthday to go out celebrating and clubbing and to have sex. Having sex with him was all that I wanted to do and a few weeks later I found out that I was pregnant.

The father of my child wanted nothing to do with me, after all, I was a child and he was a grown man with other responsibilities. He had another woman who was taking care of him. He had a family and children that I knew nothing about and he had not only lied to me about his age, but where he lived and where he worked. I came to realize that our ten minutes of lust and inappropriate meetups were not real and I had to accept that the father of my child wouldn't be around to help me raise her.

I will never forget how lost I felt during my junior year of high school, following the birth of my daughter. I was now faced with caring for a newborn baby and the possibility of not being able to graduate on time with classmates. Sure, I'd missed six weeks away from school to have my daughter, but that wasn't the real problem. I had completed all of my assignments while I was away, and before that, I'd never even skipped a class. I returned to school after my daughter was born and was certain that I was on track to graduate, that is, until I was walking down the hall and overheard a conversation between one of the counselors and a senior who was preparing for graduation. The counselor advised the student that she needed to review her academic requirements to ensure she had the required credits to graduate on time. It clicked immediately that I had no idea what my status was even though I was half way through my junior year and was supposed to be graduating the following June. It was at that moment that something on the inside of me was motivated to find out where I stood as far as graduation was concerned.

I hurried to my counselor's office and asked that she check my files and let me know where I stood. My counselor searched my files and discovered a huge error. My records showed that I'd missed taking Chemistry, Algebra, American History, and World History, all courses required to graduate. I was confused why, somehow, this had been overlooked. Aside from showing up every day and passing my classes, no one had ever informed me of what was required to graduate. I didn't understand how this could have happened?

My counselor had no answers and neither did anyone else. Devastated, I pleaded with her to do something, but she explained that it was out of her control. What was done was done and I had less than a year to make up the four mandatory courses in addition to my present course schedule, on top of being a new mother.

I was angry because this meant I might not be able to graduate on time with my peers, and it wasn't even my fault. It was the school's negligence that led to this error, not mine. No one had ever talked to me about my class selection or academic requirements. I'd trusted my counselor and school administrators to provide me with what I needed. I know now, I should have been more aware of my own academic progress, but at the time I hadn't even thought about it. I was just going to the classes I was assigned to attend.

The only solution the counselor provided was for me to attend summer school – summer school with a six-month-old infant. I didn't want to hear that. I didn't want to accept it. It was hard enough for me to accept that I was sixteen with a baby, but having to swallow the fact that I'd have to attend summer school, when I thought I was doing everything right was devastating. Still, I knew I had to take some responsibility for my life if I wanted a positive outcome.

I decided to take control of the situation, so I talked to my parents about paying for summer school and I was determined to show up to class every day. My mom did not make it easy for me. She made me take my daughter with me to summer school every day. It was embarrassing, but I was still determined. Every morning, I packed up my six-month-old baby girl and we headed out to school on the bus. I knew I had to do what was necessary to graduate on time. I accepted my responsibilities, despite my frustrations, and continued to press forward to achieve my desired results.

In order to get to a place of acceptance in my life, I had to first get clarity and understanding of what had happened and what my options were. Gaining clarity allowed me to digest and accept being a teenage mother and the information my counselor shared with me. Next, I had to take control by taking full responsibility of my daughter and talking to my parents about summer school and establishing a plan of action. Then, I had to take action by registering for the courses, and finally, I had to show up in order to complete the classes to get my diploma and graduate on time.

This same determination and motivation applies to any obstacle life throws your way. You have to practice acceptance and understand that the better you learn to accept what is, the more stress-free your life will be. Fighting against what you can't control can lead to stress, high blood pressure, and affect your overall physical and mental health. You have to learn to trust in and rely confidently on the Lord with all your heart, and not rely on your own insight or understanding.

I didn't know God then as I do now, but I am thankful He graced me with the ability to accept certain situations and not allow them to break me. When we take the time to breathe, meditate, and wait on the Lord he will make our paths straight and keep us in perfect peace. We have to learn to accept the will of God for our lives and understand that all things work together for our good in spite of what it may look like according to Romans 8:28.

"And we know [with great confidence] that God [who is deeply concerned about us] causes all things to work together [as a plan] for good for those who love God, to those who are called according to His plan and purpose"(AMP).

I have learned to accept what is and what will be. I have learned to lean not to my own understanding, but in everything trust God. I am often reminded that our lives are already ordered and predestined by the Lord. There is nothing new, the only thing that changes is our view of people, places, things, and situations. This is why acceptance is essential to our ability to B.R.E.A.T.H.E.

PRAYER OF ACCEPTANCE

Father, thank you for accepting me as your child. Thank you for clarity and understanding of who I am, and the purpose and plan that You have for my life. You are Alpha and Omega, the author and finisher of my faith. Thank you for the courage and strength to accept people, places and things that are out of my control.

Father, You are the Supreme Authority - a God of order. You have instituted other authority structures that will support healthy relationships and maintain harmony. It is my decision to surrender my will to You, that I might find protection and dwell in the secret place of the Most High.

Father, when I feel that my life is spiraling out of control, I bind my mind to the mind of Christ, and my emotions to the control of the Holy Spirit. I lose my mind from obsessive thought patterns that try to confuse me.

Obedience is far better than sacrifice. Father, You are much more interested in my listening to You than in my offerings of material things to You. Lord I want to follow You. I put away my own desires and conveniences. I yield my desires that are not in Your plan for me. Even in the midst of my fear, I surrender and entrust my future to You. I submit to the control and direction of the Holy Spirit whom You have sent to dwell in me. I am Your child. All to You I surrender. I am an overcomer by the blood of the Lamb and by the word of my testimony. I ask for all of these things or better in Jesus name. Amen.

SCRIPTURE REFERENCES

1 Corinthians 14:33	Psalm 51:6,7	1 Timothy 2:2
Colossians 1:13, 14	Psalm 91:1	Matthew 10:38-39
1 Peter 5:5 AMP	John 16;33	Matthew 6:10

REFLECTIONS

5

T – *Take Action*

Have you ever thought about what it looks and feels like to be secure in every area of your life? Do you understand what it means to be satisfied, fulfilled and set apart by God? In this chapter, our focus will be getting you to that place of satisfaction, helping you to understand the complexity of who you are and who you were created to be in this world. It is my hope that after reading this chapter you will have the necessary tools to take the action required so that you can be secure in understanding that when God made you, he made you completely equipped, nothing missing, nothing lacking. I want you to know that without a shadow of doubt you can be satisfied and fulfilled when you reset your thinking. I want you to start thinking from a sufficient mindset instead of a deficit mindset. I want you to take action by focusing your attention and your actions on being the best version of yourself that you can be.

At the end of this chapter, I want you declaring that you are secure, satisfied, and set apart. You will know who you are and whose you are.

Now in order for you to get to a place where you can make this bold declaration, you'll need to take action in the following eight areas of your life: Spiritual, Relationships, Networking, Financial, Physical, Nature, Body and Self.

Your spirituality is the first area of your life that I want you to take action in. Why you may ask? In Genesis 2:7, it states, *"The Lord God formed the man from the dust of the ground and breathed into his nostrils the breath of life, and the man became a living being."*

The Hebrew word for "living being" is *nephesh*, often translated as "soul." The point at which Adam became *nephesh* is when God joined his body (dust) and spirit (breath) together. Adam was not a living human being until he had both material (physical) and immaterial (spiritual) components. Thus, the essence of humanity is not just body, but *spirit joined with body.* Therefore, we must set aside time to develop our spirituality.

Spirituality comes by having a relationship with God. You have to be connected to the one who created you. Think of it this way, when you purchase a new car, the first place you reference to figure out how things work is the operator's manual. You search inside the manual to find out how the car turns on and off, what certain indicator lights mean, where the fuse box is; you need to know all of these things in order to properly use your vehicle. Likewise, we were created in the image of God for his purpose to be manifested on earth. We are the vehicles that God uses to do his work on earth. When you don't understand your purpose or how things are working out this is when your relationship with God and your spirituality helps to guide you in God's direction.

Instead of accepting a life filled with drama, doom and gloom, you can always go to the creator to get instruction. God created you to experience heaven on earth. In order for you operate effectively and live the abundant life you've been promised, you must open your owner's manual, the Bible, to see what God has to say about who you are and how you are to live. This is the why of spirituality. Spirituality is about relationship, not religion. For you to grow spiritually and live the best life, you have to have a relationship with God.

Ask yourself: How is my relationship with God? Do I intentionally set aside time to spend reading his Word each day? Do I spend any time with God at all during the day? Do I have a spiritual mentor? If you have answered no to any of these questions, I want you to take action by first developing a consistent time of the day that you will commit to developing your spiritual awareness. This could be through meditation, scripture memorization, praying, singing, giving God praise and all out worship. These are things that draw us closer to God. In this closeness, we are strengthened and it's confirmed that we do not have to figure life out on our own.

Proverbs 3:5-7, says, "Trust God from the bottom of your heart; don't try to figure out everything on your own. Listen for God's voice in everything you do, everywhere you go; he's the one who will keep you on track. Don't assume that you know it all." (MSG)

The second area that I want you to examine is your relationships, the people you're intimately connected to. These people can be family, parents, siblings, children, and romantic relationships. Your personal relationships shape who you are, who you are becoming and what you believe about yourself. Having healthy relationships in your life is essential to your personal growth and development to the B.R.E.A.T.H.E. journey. You don't have time for toxic relationships. Every relationship you have should build you and help make you better. Learn to walk with people who you're in agreement with, who share your vision and goals in life.

You can examine your relationships by looking at the five closest people to you or the five people you interact with the most on a weekly basis. What are their beliefs? Do you share the same faith? Do you share the same culture, vocation, profession? What are your connections to them? Do they add to your life? Do you feel depleted after you talk with them? Do you feel uplifted and energized? You want to make sure you are in relationships that help you grow and glow. Focus on nurturing and creating a community of people that understand you and support your vision. Amos 3:3 says, "Do two people walk hand in hand if they aren't going to the same place." (MSG)

The third area that I want you to examine is your network. And by network I mean the extended body of people outside of your inner circle. People you do business with, your colleagues, partnerships, clients, members of your church, and the social groups you're involved in. Having a viable network of people that you can reach out to is essential to your professional growth and development.

It is also important to consider diversifying your network. Ask yourself if your network needs to change in order for you to move forward. Be social. Get out and meet new people by attending conferences, seminars, workshops, and events where you can engage and connect. Connect with people who share ideas outside your professional area of experience in order to increase your exposure and awareness to new concepts. Tweak your networks regularly to make room for people who add value to your life. Your network should be constantly evolving.

Consider this, "Without consultation and wise advice, plans are frustrated, But with many counselors they are established and succeed." (Proverbs 15:22, AMP)

The fourth area that I want you to examine is your finances. Examine your habits, how you spend, save, and invest money. Do you have life insurance? Do you pay tithes? Give offerings or give to charity? What is your relationship with your money?

If you have an unhealthy relationship with money, you will never create the abundance you wish you had. In order to change

your

financial world, you need to change the way you think, feel, and act about money. Your finances is an area that you must manage in order to master. You cannot enjoy a life of quality without money. Take action by being clear about spending habits, investments, savings, and budgeting.

Do you have a budget? Are you tracking your income? What are you doing to create multiple streams of income? Are you being wasteful with your money? Are you fiscally responsible? To experience life in abundance you have to plan for it. Take the first step by checking your credit score.

Your credit score is a reflection of your decisions, your relationship with money and your beliefs about money. These numbers may not seem important, however, they reflect your ability to manage money and pay back debts on time. It also says to potential investors and financial backers that you are worth the investment and you have the ability to be a good steward because you've shown that you can manage what you've already been given.

Next, think about your net worth. Your net worth is what you have accumulated over time, such as, investments, stocks, real estate, and businesses. I understand that getting your finances in order is no easy feat. I come from struggle. I come from living paycheck to paycheck. Struggling does not feel good. It does not feel good to go into a store and not have enough money to feed your children or and pay your bills. I also come from a family of hustlers so I know how to generate money, but I was not taught how to save it and manage it. I had to change my mindset around money.

My pastor teaches to owe no man anything. To pay for everything in cash and as a result of that teaching and the small shift in my relationship with money, I no longer have credit card debt. I'm also, on a three year plan to pay my car off and a five year plan to pay my mortgage and student loan debt off. Because I turned my attention to building my finances, I was able to take my children with me on the B.R.E.A.T.H.E. Cruise for a week on the Royal Caribbean's Anthem of the Seas. This was a $5,000 cruise. And I share this, not to brag, but to encourage you so that you can see what's possible and how when you use money as a tool it can help you to create enjoyable memories with your family and live a debt free life.

Look at your bank account to see where money is being drained or waisted. Are you planning ahead with your money? What does your financial portfolio look like? A great tool to help you get started or keep you on track is Mint.com. It's an awesome resource that allows you to see all of your money in one number according to the information that you input, which can help you determine your net worth. Think of your net worth as everything you have minus everything you owe. Enter in all of your financial information and Mint.com will do the math and show you how to save and invest to keep your net worth growing.

I have been studying the mindset of wealthy people for the last three years. Did you know that wealthy people think differently about money than average people. Wealthy people plan 10, 15, and 20 years out. Wealthy people plan for their profits and their philanthropic work. Average people plan for the next 30 days because their focus is on survival. Wealthy people believe that poverty is the root of all evil, while average people believe that you have to become something to get rich like a business owner or CEO. Wealthy people believe in living below their means not above their means. And average people believe that they have to work for someone else to make money. Wealthy people teach their children how to save, how to thrive, and how to leverage resources, and relationships. Average people lack the knowledge to teach their children how to accumulate wealth. I challenge you to be aware of your financial status and make conscious decisions when it comes to your finances.

First Timothy 6: 17-19 confirms, *"As for the rich in this present world, instruct them not to be conceited and arrogant, nor to set their hope on the uncertainty of riches, but on God, who richly and ceaselessly provides us with everything for our enjoyment. Instruct them to do good, to be rich in good works, to be generous, willing to share [with others]. In this way storing up for themselves the enduring riches of a good foundation for the future, so that they may take hold of that which is truly life."*

The fifth area that I want you to examine is your physical environment. Your physical environment includes your home, car, furnishings, where you work, all things that are around you. Designers, architects, and people concerned with interior spaces, and human interaction understand that the construct of spaces and environments impact people's thinking and behavior. This past summer I was introduced to Feng Shui in order to help me create good energy in my classroom in a non-traditional charter school where I teach during the day.

A large percentage of the student body are teen parents, homeless, hungry, displaced, or in and out of the DHS system. It was important for me to create a warm and welcoming environment for these students and a space that was conducive for learning. One of my colleagues allowed me to borrow two of her Feng Shui books on creating energy and using color in different spaces. I used them and added my personal touch to design my classroom, and as a result, I have seen changed behaviors, moods, and productivity in the students and in those who come to visit.

Your workspace is your home away from home. It's the place where you fight for market share, pursue new business opportunities, and realize your dreams. It's also, for better or for worse, part of the public face of your company. When I was designing both my living and classroom space, it was very important to me that people felt welcomed as soon as they opened the door. I ensured every wall was off white with a splash of color in the room. I made sure that the color of the furniture accented the overall ambiance of the work space. I needed the energy in every room to feel positive and welcoming. I used the color chart below to help me choose what colors to add. I chose purple because it represents abundance. I chose green because it represents health. I chose yellow because it represents balance, and blue because it represents wisdom and knowledge.

According to Feng Shui, the front door of any area should be in perfect condition as it represents wealth. To draw the energy to your front door, place a beautiful plant and light either side of the door. The hall represents opportunities, therefore, ensure it's kept clutter free so that the energy can circulate. To activate the beneficial chi in the hall, place a beautiful mirror and fresh flowers. Fresh flowers instantly uplift the energy of a space. Place coats and shoes inside a closed cupboard so they don't stagnate the energy. The kitchen is a vital space as its energy represents nourishment and relationship harmony for the occupants. Ensure that the furniture for the living room the room where you entertain and spend time with your family and friends is in proportion to the space. Do not block any doors with furniture and position the main sofa against a wall to provide the occupants with support. To activate wealth energy place a lamp in the corner of the room (diagonally opposite the room door). To encourage a restful sleep, the bedrooms must be a light neutral color and the beds must have a headboard and be positioned with the headboard against a solid wall. Ideally, the bed must not be in line with the bedroom door. Place side tables either side of the bed to provide support.

Remember, your environment matters. You create your environment with your words, so include positive affirmations throughout your space with pictures. Speak into existence what you envision for your future. I have used all of the mentioned concepts in my own home and workspace to create my desired environment, and it allows me to work, laugh, and create. I have a sense of peace at the beginning and end of my day. In order for you to create your desired environment you must write the vision, picture it, and use positive affirmations to create your vision. Start with Habakkuk 2:2-3, "Write this. Write what you see. Write it out in big block letters so that it can be read on the run. This vision-message is a witness pointing to what's coming. It aches for the coming—it can hardly wait! And it doesn't lie. If it seems slow in coming, wait. It's on its way. It will come right on time." (MSG)

The sixth area is self. Self is everything that makes you who you are. Your beliefs, talents, your unique purpose, your why, how you move in this world. Think about what God created you to do, what the world can expect from you based on who God created you to be and do. Take this time to pause and think about how you have been moving about in this world. I know for me, sometimes, I am super confident, committed, and faithful to the vision that God has given me, but at other times I feel overwhelmed and I begin to doubt the vision, but only for a second. I don't stay in defeat or despair for long. I realized that with self-awareness, I can stand guard over my mind and return to the confident me committed to God's vision for my life.

Part of building self is guarding your mind. I can look back over my life and see the patterns of inconsistent thinking. When I thought low of myself and felt overwhelmed, I tended to be scattered in my thinking and be all over the place. I was doing so much, but without results.

I knew I had to make a shift in my thinking so that I could consistently attract the things, resources, and people that I desired. I had to eliminate the lie that I wasn't enough. Even as an adult, I've been told that I am too bold and outspoken, but I know better than to allow the opinions of others to shape the way I think about or view myself. I have learned to overcome negative thoughts and a deficit mindset by replacing those negative thoughts with positive affirmations and renewing my mind with the Word of God. I became intentional about my emotional intelligence. I was honest with myself and took responsibility for my actions and habits that did not align with the results that I wanted to achieve.

Place things around you that remind you of what you want. What are good visuals to remind you of where you're going? Place affirmations all throughout your environment to remind you of who you are and whose you are. For example, over my bed some of my affirmations are, *Everything and everyone prospers me every day in every way now. Money cometh to me easily and effortlessly. Greater achievements are coming in spite of what I see.* These remind me not to look at or focus on the things that I don't have right now. These affirmations encourage me and keep me active in what I allow myself to focus on.

Are you owning the results you are creating? Are you owning how you make people feel? Are you owning what you love and what you don't love? Are you owning the greatness in you? Are you taking responsibility for the contribution you give to the world for the way you show up as everyone's superwomen? Are you taking full responsibility for your life? Your life is a physical manifestation of the conversation that is going on in your head. Evict the thoughts that are not supporting your destiny.

As you move forward, remember that your words have power and part of bettering yourself is by being more specific and calculated with your words and what you speak over your own life. You can create your own positive affirmations just by making sure that nothing but positivity flows from your mouth. Take note, Proverbs 18:21 says, "Death and life are in the power of the tongue, And those who love it *and* indulge it will eat its fruit *and* bear the consequences of their words." (AMP)

The seventh area that I want you to examine is your diet. One of the factors in having a healthy body is what we eat. Eating is one of the great pleasures of life. More than just a basic need, eating brings together family and friends and is also about community and fellowship. In enjoying good food, many forget that your health depends greatly on your diet. It is crucial you pay close attention to what you put into your body. What you eat impacts your health, energy and vitality.

I have struggled with staying healthy for the last fifteen years of my life. As a young person I was very skinny and everyone teased me. So as a child I was constantly told to eat, but I never gained weight no matter what I ate. I remember my family members would make me drink nutritional supplements such as Ensure in order for me to put weight on. It's safe to say that as a result of my childhood experience I developed unhealthy eating habits as a teen and as an adult. The weight didn't start to stick to me until after I had my third child when I was twenty-five. By this time in my life, I had developed food allergies and I was very sick all of the time. I remember from 25 to 30 I could not hold anything down. Everything I ate seemed liked it upset my stomach. I would have diarrhea and cramping for days. It was so bad that I would have to keep plastic bags in my car because I could not make it to the bathroom when driving from one destination to the next. I was exhausted all the time and I often felt depleted and lethargic.

In 2007, one of my client's mother was an herbalist and made me a stomach formula. She told me that I could no longer eat spicy, fried, greasy, or sweet foods. I had to take the stomach formula before every meal in order for me not to get stomach cramps or have to take anti-diarrhea medicine. I did not know at the time that I was allergic to sugar and a ton of other things that are in almost everything that I enjoyed eating. I would sometimes only eat one meal a day because of how sick I felt. My poor eating habits were preventing me from enjoying public outings with my family and other important events. I knew I couldn't continue on like this and I had to take what I was putting into my body more seriously.

When I finally started to think about what I was feeding my body and cut out the foods that were making me sick, I started having a better quality of life and I was filled with more energy. I gained confidence in attending social events and creating meaningful memories with my children by being able to attend their games and school activities. I was able to become more present in my life and really enjoy the world that was happening around me.

Think about the foods that you eat, how does your body respond to the foods you consume? Are you bloated, gassy? Do you have irritable bowels? Are you eliminating after each meal? Are you constipated? Look at the amount of fluid you drink? Is what you're eating or drinking giving you energy? What are you putting in to your body?

Matthew 12:33 says, "If you grow a healthy tree, you'll pick healthy fruit. If you grow a diseased tree, you'll pick worm-eaten fruit. The fruit tells you about the tree." (MSG)

The eighth area that I want you to examine is your access to nature. Being in touch with nature slows things down and allows us to see things we take for granted. Take action by becoming aware of community spaces. Spending more time outdoors nurtures our "nature neurons" and our natural creativity. For example, at the University of Michigan, researchers demonstrated that after just an hour interacting with nature, memory performance and attention spans improved by 20%. In workplaces designed with nature in mind, employees are more productive and take less sick time.

Pennsylvania researchers found that patients in rooms with tree views had shorter hospitalizations, needed less pain medication and fewer negative comments in the nurses' notes, compared to patients with views of brick. Researchers in Sweden have found joggers who exercise in a natural green setting feel more restored and less anxious, angry, or depressed than people who burn the same amount of calories jogging in a built urban setting.

Last summer, I made a commitment to walk one mile after work each day and it changed my productivity. That one mile each day renewed me, refueled me, and revived me. I love green grass, beautiful ocean blue water and sand under my feet. I enjoy walking and bike riding with my children. Being outside and feeling the cool breeze of fall or the gentle breeze of summer brings an unexplainable calmness. The outdoors immediately refuels me and re-energizes me. It is an immediate pick me up for my mood and attitude. Being outside makes me feel grateful for the things that I have, my children and family.

Don't be afraid to bring some nature into your personal space. Place plants in your home to provide more oxygen in your home environment. I challenge you to go outside and become one with nature, find local public spaces where you can run, walk, jog, ride a bike, or go on a hike. This will heighten your senses and give you clarity in your thinking and a sense of enjoyment. Nature was created for our overall physical and mental health.

You now have the necessary tools to take the action required so that you can be secure in understanding that when God made you, he made you completely equipped, nothing missing, nothing lacking. I want you to know that without a shadow of doubt you can be satisfied and fulfilled when you reset your thinking. I want you to start thinking from a sufficient mindset instead of a deficient mindset. I want you to take action by focusing your attention and your actions on being the best version of yourself that you can be.

PRAYER OF TAKING ACTION

> I purpose to live according to the Holy Spirit, I set my mind on and seek those things which gratify the Holy Spirit. I no longer live my life after the flesh. I live the life of the Holy Spirit. Holy Spirit direct and control me. May I always be a doer of the Word. I have God's wisdom and I draw it forth in prayer. I am strong in the Lord and in the power of His hands.

In Christ, I am filled with the Godhead; Father Son, Holy Spirit. I ask for all of these things or better in Jesus name. Amen.

SCRIPTURE REFERENCES

Romans 8:2,4,9,14,31,37 AMP James 3:17 AMP Romans 12:21

Hebrews 13:5 Ephesians 6:10 James 1:22

REFLECTIONS

6

H – *Heal*

Did you know that there are three degrees of burns and each degree requires a different level of care? The same is true for emotional healing. There are different levels of hurt and pain, and each level requires different treatment. For example, first degree burns extend only on the epidermis, the top layer of our skin, and cause reddening and pain. These are considered minor health issues and are commonly treated with self-care like immersion in cool water, aloe, or other types of soothing applicants. Just the same, emotional hurt requires self-care, as well. When we hear hurtful things like, "You're stupid or no one will ever want you. You are ignorant, fat, lazy, ugly, etc." over time, we begin to believe those lies. We all experience pain in life, whether emotional or physical pain. But God promises that there is a purpose in the pain that we experience. We can press on each day knowing that our God loves us and wants to use the hurt and pain in this world to bring Him glory.

Consider Hebrews 12:2 to help you understand the purpose of pain in your life and encourage you to find joy in the middle of painful situations. The Word says,

> *"Looking unto Jesus the author and finisher of our faith;*
> *who for the joy that was set before him endured the cross,*
> *despising the shame, and is set down at the right hand of*
> *the throne of God."*

Second degree burns penetrate to the dermis, the layer beneath the skin, causing pain and redness, but also causing blisters and skin thickening. These types of burns are treated with self-care like antibiotics and loose gauze to protect the wounded area. Like the loss of a close friend or betrayal from someone you trusted, second degree emotional pain goes deeper than the surface level of offense or arguments.

Healing from this emotional pain requires self-care in the form of self-acceptance and self-love. You have to guard your heart in a positive manner to be mindful of what you're exposed to. If you are not careful your burn will not heal properly and this could lead to an infection which will lead to more physical and emotional pain as well as discomfort. You have to allow God to heal you where you hurt. For his Word says in Psalms 147:3 3, "He heals the brokenhearted and binds up their wounds." (MSG)

Third-degree burns are more severe. They destroy the dermis and the epidermis and affect deeper tissue. Third-degree burns result in white or blackened charred skin that may be lose feeling and functionality. The healing process for third degree burns may require major surgical repair, lifelong assistive care, support groups, and counselors. A third-degree burn may feel like the pain of a divorce, rape, molestation, domestic violence, rejection, or other types of emotional pain. These types of pain both physical and emotional can leave you feeling numb until you are unrecognizable like blackened and charred skin. The healing process for emotional third degree pain requires forgiveness in addition to the support of a group or counseling so that you are not alone to face your issues head on and move forward.

In order for healing to begin, we must first identify the pain, determine where it came from and assess how deep it is. My hurt began early in my childhood. I had trust issues that stemmed from the relationship that I had with my mother, my family members, and my childhood friends. I was first hurt because my mother did not raise me. I lived with my great grandmother until the age of 10. We lived in a roach infested two-bedroom row home in the projects of South Philadelphia, where I always had to share a room. My great grandmother provided for all of her own children, her grandchildren, and her great grandchildren from her social security check that she received once a month. There were three generations under one roof.

After I turned 10, I began to live with my mother off and on with her friends; our housing was never stable. I know now that she did the best that she could, but I did not understand that as a child. My friends' parents were always doing things with them and taking them places and I yearned for those quality interactions with my mother. But as a result of my mother's own struggles with life coupled with physical and verbal abuse from her mother, she moved a lot and I would stay with friends and families. I felt abandoned and neglected at times, and the treatment from other family members, such as uncles, cousins, and aunts, didn't help the feeling of abandonment. The worst part was my cousins who would take me everywhere and expose me to things that weren't age appropriate like adult movies, parties, drugs, and alcohol. I was their guinea pig and I spent many years with peers who I thought were my friends, but I never felt accepted.

With feelings of abandonment and the negative attention from my cousins, I felt like I was always trying to fit in. As I got older, I started looking for love in all of the wrong places and I consistently found myself in unhealthy relationships with both men and women. I wanted to be accepted and I called any and everyone, who showed me attention my friend. My mom would always say, "Just because they smile in your face does not make them a friend." But, I didn't hear her. I just wanted to be loved and accepted.

Unfortunately, it was some of my own family members, such as my great- aunt, who introduced my mother and other family members to alcohol, weed, and crack. Her house was the party house. Any and everything went down at my great-aunt's house. I don't remember there being any rules in her house. My aunt always made sure everyone had something to eat, drink, and smoke regardless of your age. I can remember her giving me beer to sip around the age of five. My great-aunt along with my uncles, mother, and cousins were always selling something. Everyone had a hustle. This is how they survived and what went on in their house, stayed in their house good, bad, or indifferent. This was the only rule, not to tell the family business.

As a result of growing up in a family of hustlers, I learned how to get to a dollar early. I sold ice cream on the corner of my grandmother's block. I cut grass, sold incense, socks, and oils from the back of my godfather's trunk. By 13, I learned how to do hair and styled everyone's finger waves and braids. I always had money from my various hustles. But, my family and some people I called friends only wanted to spend my money. There was no reciprocation. I was the one always giving and they were the ones always taking.

My family was also not very supportive. We only got together as a family for weddings and funerals. My mom always told me to accept the reality that my family would never support me because they never supported her. I did not understand that growing up and it used to really hurt me. I could not process why I came from a dysfunctional family and I wanted what I thought all of my peers had.

In addition to that, everyone in my family had an addiction to something. I watched their unhealthy relationships and I observed how they used and manipulated everyone in their lives for their own selfish gain. I grew up with female cousins who were married to men who had girlfriends on the side. I grew up with an uncle who was a pimp and had prostitutes around me all of the time. I watched them get dressed and go into the street to sell their bodies. I had another married uncle who slept with anything moving. I don't think I had one example of a healthy relationship from anyone in my family. I came to realize, they were all functional addicts.

As a result of the unhealthy relationships I witnessed as a child, I became familiar and comfortable with people who didn't have good intentions. My childhood experience with a dysfunctional family led me to believe as an adult that this dysfunctional life was normal. This lie that I believed then resulted in me marrying a man who I knew had a drug addiction. At first, I thought, his addiction couldn't be that serious. Based on my experience with my mother and other family members, I believed that I could save my husband even change him. I stayed because I wanted my marriage to work, but digging deeper into the wound, I realized that I was suffering from a third degree burn.

The reality is when we don't heal from our past, history repeats itself and continues to show up in other relationships just like a burn that has healed or received proper treatment. As my marriage was falling apart, I started to take a hard look at myself and my choices and I was able to see how deep my burns actually were.

My healing journey started before I decided to end my marriage and it started with first identifying the root of my pain. I'd never dealt with the pain from my childhood. I'd only buried it under a dysfunctional marriage. I recognized that even though I wasn't getting the love I thought I needed from anyone, God was still present and He still loved me. It was then, in December of 2013, that I made the decision to love myself and to take action steps to begin to manifest healing in every area of my life.

I first started to seek God and I found the strength to get Godly counsel. I found a woman of God, who shared her own story of abuse and mistreatment with me and we built a relationship to the point that I had her on speed dial and I was able to call her anytime life was getting me down. God directed my attention, not to my family or even to my husband, but to me. I knew that I needed to start working on me.

Through years of mental and verbal torment, my self-esteem had been torn down but, it was time to let all of the pain from the past go so I could begin to heal and receive all the promises I was reading about in God's word. Once I began to receive counsel from God, I started waking up early in the morning, at 4 a.m. so that I could read Proverbs and pray. I had to start reading the Word of God to rebuild my self-esteem and grow in my faith. Reading and meditating on the Word of God as soon as I woke up, helped me to mentally be in the right state of mind. The Word of God continues to center me and help me to focus my thoughts on things that matter like seeking first the kingdom of God so that everything that I need will always be provided according to Matthew 6:33. " But seek ye first the kingdom of God, and his righteousness; and all these things shall be added unto you." (KJV)

Next, I knew that I needed support, so I decided to create my own village of supporters. In January of 2014, I posted my first 90 day challenge on Facebook to help me gain balance and begin the healing process. I created a Facebook group and publicized the challenge to help me stay accountable. It was called, "Get Healthy Mind, Body, Spirit and Financially Fit in 90 Days."

Although a lot of people did not stay the course, I still had a small group of people, who became my village, and I knew they were watching my transformation. It was about accountability and so much changed for me in those 90 days because I decided to show up. I got up at 4 a.m. every morning to prepare to present to the people who were committed to the group. I matched their commitment and showed up on Facebook every day. I was forcing myself to show up no matter what and that made me stronger with a new sense of determination and this helped me to continue to heal. I shared my vulnerable self and somedays I would even cry. After the challenge, I felt stronger, wiser, healthier, and more importantly whole enough to start healing.

Today, I maintain my healing from the inside out. I love freely and live out loud with unapologetic purpose. I recognize that healing is a continual process, a day by day journey. In order to stay healed from the hurt and pain of the past I knew I had to stay in the Word of God. Stay on top of your healing process and take care of yourself because situations will come along and attempt to reopen those old wounds and you'll be back to zero. I have to renew my mind consistently in order to continue my healing process and not become distracted.

Ending a 17-year cycle of emotional scars and experiencing every level of emotional burns, has been a journey, but today I am breathing, I am healing, and God has made me whole again. Understand that this process takes time and you have to constantly work on healing. Renewal comes with time paired with staying in God's Word.

PRAYER OF HEALING

Jesus, I thank You that You have both the power and authority to heal my body and my mind. I boldly come to You today to ask for your grace and healing power to be at work in my body and my mind. I trust that You are powerful and looking for an opportunity to show your power in me and through me.

Father, You have rescued me from the dominion of darkness and have brought me into the Kingdom of the Son of Your Love. I was in darkness, but now I walk in Your light. The abuse is exposed and reproved by your light. It is made visible and clear, and where everything is visible and clear there is light.

Help me to grow in grace, recognition, knowledge, and understanding of my Lord and Savior, Jesus Christ, so that I may experience Your love and trust You to be a Father to me. The history of my earthly family is filled with abusive behavior, hatred, strife, rage, and addiction. The painful memory of my past abuse (verbal, emotional, physical, and sexual) has caused me to be hostile and abusive to others. I break the power of stress and trauma and release your peace. I speak to every part of my body and mind and command it to be whole in Jesus' name. Function properly—the way God designed me to function.

Jesus, send your word and heal me today. You paid the price for my healing, so I trust that You are at work in me. Holy Spirit, fill every part of me with your supernatural presence. Drive out all that is not good, holy, and true. I receive the healing You have for me today.

I confess my sin of abuse, resentment, and hostility toward others, and I ask You to forgive me. You are faithful and just to forgive my sin and cleanse me from all unrighteousness. I am tired of reliving the past in my present life, perpetuating the generational curse of anger and abuse.

Lord, set a guard over my lips today and search my heart. Try me and know my thoughts. See if there is any evil way in me and lead me in the way everlasting. If there is anything in my life that displeases You, Father, remove it in Jesus's name. Circumcise my heart and cause my desires and my words to line up with Yours.

Lord I put on Your whole armor that I may be able to successfully stand against all the strategies and the tricks of the devil. I thank You that the evil power of abuse is broken, overthrown, and cast down. I submit myself to You and resist the devil. The need to hurt others no longer controls me or my family. In Jesus's name. Amen.

Scripture References

Romans 10:9	Romans 7:18-25	Matthew 6:10
1 John 1:9	Colossians 1:13 AMP	Galatians 3:13
Ephesians 5:8,13	Ephesians 6:11,12	James 4:7

REFLECTIONS

E – *Elevate*

Elevation is the action of promotion, upgrade, advancement, and the ability to rise above previous conditions. Elevation means to move forward beyond your situation and current circumstances. It means to do an about face and change your behavior, posture, attitude and disposition. Elevation looks like having abundant health and an abundant mindset.

When I think about elevation, I think about encouraging, empowering, and helping women get unstuck in every area of their lives. I think about women like my mom, family members, daughters, friends, students, and clients who were abused physically and mentally by either their spouses, parents, and others and need to be elevated out of their situations. I think about those who have been isolated, those who have been told nobody loves them, cares about them, or will support them. Spouses and parents who have told them that they were not good enough and they begin to believe that lie. They began to believe that they were all alone. I want to let these women know they are loved, cared about and that God is concerned with them.

Elevation was the next step for me. When I begin this B.R.E.A.T.H.E. journey, I needed to get in the Word of God, begin to emulate Christ, and begin to model my life as his Word instructed. I had to elevate my mindset by thinking new thoughts and focusing on the promises of God. God promises an abundant life and I shouldn't be living under my potential. John 10:10 tells us, "The thief cometh not, but for to steal, and to kill, and to destroy: I come that they might have life, and that they might have it more abundantly." (ASV)

I needed to rise above my current circumstances of being broke, broken, and bankrupt in my emotions, in my relationships, in my home, in my marriage, and also in my health and finances. I knew things had to change and I had to do something to reclaim all of these areas I had been struggling in. But on Friday, August 20, 2016, I was not prepared for what was to come, even though there had been signs majority of the year.

At the time, my husband and I owned and operated OMART Training and Development. We provided professional development training, workforce development, and consultation to those wanted to open up a daycare, individuals who wanted to work in a daycare, and child development training to schools and community based organizations. I went to pick up a monthly payment from one of our clients at the end of August 2016. This payment was almost a thousand dollars more than what we usually received. I entered the building and pressed the button to take me to the fifth floor where the fiscal office was located. Something in me didn't feel quite right and the entire time on my way there I was silently praying, "Oh Lord. I hope this check is here. I hope my husband did not intercept this check."

I reached the fifth floor, entered the office and asked the clerk if she

62

had the check. The lady stopped what she was doing and looked into my eyes. She told me that my husband had picked the check up at 8 a.m. and I was three hours too late. My heart sunk and I begin to cry on the inside, but I could not allow a tear to drop from my eyes. I looked at her, smiled, and said okay. I told her no worries and to have a good weekend. I proceeded to get back on the elevator to exit the building. My mind was all over the place, my heart was beating in my chest and tears started to roll down my eyes because I knew what this meant. I was not going to see my husband for a few days, and the mortgage was not going to get paid. The school clothes our children needed were not going to be purchased, not one bill due or person we owed was going to receive a payment, and there was not going to be any food in the house.

To my surprise, I was also informed that my husband had removed my name from the account with this client and checks were no longer being made out to the business, but they were now being made payable directly to him. At that moment, I really could not breathe, literally. I felt no air circulating or oxygen running through my body. I was numb all over, dumbfounded, and devastated all at the same time. I had no money and I was a wreck. I wanted to give up and kill myself. I contemplated drinking until I passed out, but I had to keep it together for myself and my children. As I said before, I was teetering between being a superwoman and suicide.

In order to overcome the crisis that was staring me in my face, I had to be resilient. Taking my life, and the life of anyone else for that matter, was not realistic. I had to be still, get before the Lord, and pray about my next moves. I needed courage to have a very uncomfortable conversation with my client about the condition of my business and my marriage. I was terrified of the consequences and I was embarrassed. I am a private person for the most part, however in this situation I felt naked and exposed. I had no choice, but to be transparent without negatively talking about my husband or his addiction. I was in a very difficult place and I was very uncomfortable. I knew things had to change, so I immediately sought after wise counsel. I called my mentor, a trusted advisor, and lawyer. I knew there would be safety in wise counsel, and I knew that this was not the time for me to throw in the towel, give up, walk away, or fall apart. It was time for me to take a stand. I was either going to drown from being overwhelmed, devastated, and heartbroken or elevate myself above the water that was over my head and start swimming to the top.

The following Monday came and there was no turning back, I had to meet with my client and tell them that going forward I needed them to split the check and that I was no longer working with my husband; that, in fact, we had been separated since January of the same year. That was hard, it was difficult, my palms were sweating, and I was very nervous. At that moment, I had to be a superwoman and use my superpowers of love, kindness, wisdom, and gentleness in how I dealt with my client. I could have chosen to cower in this situation, but I elevated the situation in a positive manner by focusing on the facts and making my case as to why they needed to work with me and split the checks.

I had to ask God to do surgery on my heart. The heart is significant to God because God said, "I will give you a new heart and put a new spirit in you; I will remove from you, your heart of stone and give you a heart of flesh." (Ezekiel 36:26 NIV). I needed God to do surgery on my heart within forty eight hours so that my clients did not see, feel, or sense the fear, hurt and pain that I was feeling at that time. I needed to be believable and I would not have had the strength to approach my clients that morning if God did not come through for me. Negative thoughts had crept into my mind, telling me that I was going to fail, that they wouldn't accept or respect me, that I wouldn't be able to feed my family, but it was only in spending time with God that I was able to elevate out of that deficit mentality and go into that meeting and be successful.

The enemy works overtime to ensure our lives are chaotic and confused all the time. He is always trying to tempt us and steal our peace. Knowing this, I made a decision not to go into my meeting with a victim mentality. I needed to be as bold as a lion and confident in my ability to take over the client's contract without my husband.

God's provision in this situation reminds me that we must expect the best. I can't say that enough, it is important that we learn how to expect the best, provide the best, and excel in everything that we do. It is my desire to live in abundance in every area of my life. If we sit around complaining and pointing fingers about what we should have or could have done, it's not going to change our situation.

Advocate for yourself when things don't happen, don't just accept it. It's easy to get comfortable, complacent and just do enough to get by, but we have to want more, we have to do more, we have to give more. We have to live out loud, we have to live in abundance, and we have to elevate. This is the only way we can get to our wealthy place and our healthy place of breathing. Abundance is available to every single one of us. We have to go above and beyond our own expectations and not worry about what others may think. We have to rise. We have to shine. We have to be bold. We have to be courageous. This is how we elevate ourselves! I encourage you to take the time to breathe today, no matter what is going on in your life, no matter the circumstance, you are more than enough!

Take time over the next few days to meditate over these scriptures and breathe in a new outlook of abundance.

> *""And we know that all things work together for good to them that love God, to them who are the called according to his purpose. For whom he did foreknow, he also did predestinate to be conformed to the image of his Son, that he might be the firstborn among many brethren.*
>
> *30 Moreover whom he did predestinate, them he also called: and whom he called, them he also justified: and whom he justified, them he also glorified." Romans 8:28-30 (KJV)*

We don't need anyone's stamp of approval because we are approved by our heavenly Father. Learn how to encourage yourself and cover yourself every day with the word of God. Look in the mirror put your lip gloss on and say I am made in the image of God. I love ME.

> *"Be not afraid of sudden fear, neither of the desolation of the wicked, when it cometh. For the Lord shall be thy confidence, and shall keep thy foot from being taken." Proverbs 3:25-27 (KJV)*

Now that you are fully equipped, it's time to elevate. Take everything you've learned here and don't sit on it, but instead materialize it, execute it! Don't delay in elevating your mind to accept the positive changes for your self-improvement. Stay elevated by continuing to study the Word of God and keeping your focus on the important developments going on in your life. Elevate your life, elevate your health, elevate your thinking, and elevate your mindset. Elevate everything around you because when you begin to do so, guess what, you will begin to attract all those good things that you want. Rise above current negative mindsets and circumstances, make the conscious effort to B.R.E.A.T.H.E.

PRAYER OF ELEVATION

Father, I pray for everyone that reads this book and shares this book. Help us to remain teachable that we may receive instructions from our spiritual leaders, mentors, and accountability partners. We are Your children and You have equipped us for the work of ministry, for the edifying of the body of Christ. Bring us to the unity of faith and knowledge of the son of God, to a perfect man, to the measure of the stature of the fullness of Christ.

On the authority of Your Word, we declare we are more than conquerors and are gaining a surpassing victory through Christ Jesus who loves us. We refuse to let ourselves be overcome by evil, but we will overcome evil with good. We have on the full armor of light, love and peace, clothed with the Lord Jesus Christ, and make no provision for indulging our flesh.

May we always be doers of God's Word. We have God's wisdom, and we draw it forth with prayer. We are peace-loving, full of compassion and good fruits. We are free from doubts, wavering, and insincerity. We are subject to God, our father.

We are strong in the Lord and in the power of His might. Therefore, we take our stand against the devil and resist him; he flees from us. We draw close to God and God draws close to us. We do not fear, for God

never leaves us. We ask for all of these things or better
in Jesus name. Amen.

Scripture References

Romans 12:21	Hebrews 13:5	Colossians 2:10
James 3:17	James 1:22	James 4:7,8

REFLECTIONS

FINAL WORDS FOR THE JOURNEY

It is my desire that you elevate from wherever you are in your life to a place of abundance so that you live a stress-free life and B.R.E.A.T.H.E. The B.R.E.A.T.H.E. journey includes you creating a healthy village for yourself, surrounding yourself with like-minded people who will help you stay accountable for walking in purpose and being great. You don't need negative people, places, or things in your space and in your environment. You must release, let go, and take control in order to survive. You're worth it and your life matters. You are a difference maker. You will begin to attract people who understand you and want to support you. You will begin to attract people who actually want to pour into you, give to you, and help you reach your fully elevated potential.

Above all, you must remember that the journey of self-development is a process. On paper, things sometimes seem easy until we begin to try and walk in our new found revelation. Although the road to B.R.E.A.T.H.E is not a smooth and straight path, rest assured that God is with you along the way. If you stumble and fall, it's okay. This journey is about consistently renewing your mind and remembering to B.R.E.A.T.H.E.

When you feel that you need a motivational boost, don't be afraid to revisit the principles you've learned here. You may even find new ways to implement some of the strategies you learned along the way. Believe in yourself, value yourself, and see how, not only your perspective changes, but how people around you treat you because of your confidence. Believe that you are beautiful inside and out and that you lack nothing, you are fully equipped to handle anything that comes at you.

When you begin to feel that people around you may not have your best interest at heart, remember it's okay to release toxic people and toxic relationships. You don't have to feel stressed out or suffocated by interactions that do not add to your life or hinder you from reaching your full potential. Again, it's not an easy task, but prayer, fasting, and obedience to God's Word are the tools you need to get through it all.

Relinquishing familiar, but toxic, relationships is difficult to overcome, but once you've taken out the trash, so to speak, you're ready to embrace this season of newness. Everyday you wake up, you have the opportunity to move on from past mistakes, even the ones from yesterday. Focus on the future and the life that you are working to create for yourself. Embrace the transition of these changes and leave negative things, such as, stress, frustration, and anxiety behind.

Moving on is no easy feat and neither is acceptance, but the two work hand in hand. When we learn acceptance it allows us to see things from a different perspective. Accept responsibility for mistakes, but don't hold those mistakes against yourself, press forward and accept those mistakes as learning experiences. Think back to meditating on God's Word day and night so that your mind and heart can accept things you don't control and people you can't change.

Now you're ready to take control. Take action to focus your attention on what's important, being the best version of yourself. Taking control is about feeling secure and satisfied in yourself. Review the eight areas of your life where you can begin to take control of today. Spirituality, relationships, networks, finances, environment, diet, nature and self are all areas that need your personal attention to be able to help you continue this journey. While each takes time to develop, it is well worth it to spend time consciously making an effort to work on each area to improve your life.

Along the way, you will find yourself healing from old wounds that seemed to never close. Don't continue to believe the lies of those old wounds. Find support in healing through groups and even counseling to help you get through this part of the journey and keep you focused on your personal growth.

Your Sister in the Journey called B.R.E.A.T.H.E.

Obioma Martin

Connect with me on social media
FB@obiomamartin,
IG@Iamobiomamartin,
Twitter @Iamobiomamartin
Youtube@Iamobiomamartin

One-on-one and group coaching is available.

To book me to speak at your next event, bible study, youth group, conference, simply shoot me an email at obioma@obiomamartin.com

And, be sure to visit my website to stay current with events, tour dates, products and services. www.obiomamartin.com.

ABOUT THE AUTHOR

Obioma Martin is an inspirational speaker, accountability-coach, author, small business expert, childcare consultant and esteemed advocate for women's empowerment. Martin's passion for equipping women with the tools they need to, not only survive but, prosper and live audaciously, has launched her into a life of unparalleled servitude, wherein she continues to thrive by helping others.

She is the founder of several organizations that serve the underserved in the community: OMAX Institute which provides: professional development, mentoring, and coaching to childcare providers, OMART -Women Supporting Women, which supports survivors of domestic abuse and provides opportunities for them to start businesses and return to school, and Obioma Martin, LLC which supports entrepreneurs across all industries in the areas of consulting, accountability coaching, and public speaking.

Martin has helped over 3000 women get off welfare and get the credentials required to complete and further their education. A life-long learner herself, Martin holds multiple degrees: associates degree in Early Childhood Education, bachelors in Childcare Management, a master's degree in Early Childhood Education and Leadership and she is also a Goldman Sachs 10,000 Small Business Program alumnus. Martin is currently one class away from being a certified biblical counselor and will be starting her doctoral studies in organizational leadership in the fall 2018.

Martin is the author of several accountability journals that guide, both men and women, through the process of getting unstuck in every area of their lives. In her latest release, *B.R.E.A.T.H.E.- Empowered to*

Live a Stress-Free Life, Martin shares her stories of hardships, overcoming life's obstacles and the thin line strong women often teeter between superhero and suicide. This gripping composition walks readers through a journey of self-discovery and self-development and brings them out at the end elevated, empowered, and equipped to live their best lives.